The Foolish Son

Written by Amy Norris
Illustration by Alexis Olguin & Amy Norris

There once was a boy
A foolish old soul
Who settled his family
Right next to a hole

He dug it himself
This cavern he made
He dug it in secret
With each passing day
He dug in the night
While his family lay sleeping
While all were away to the
Hole he went creeping

On occasion he wanted
To let the secret all out
But the thought left him trembling
With fear and with doubt

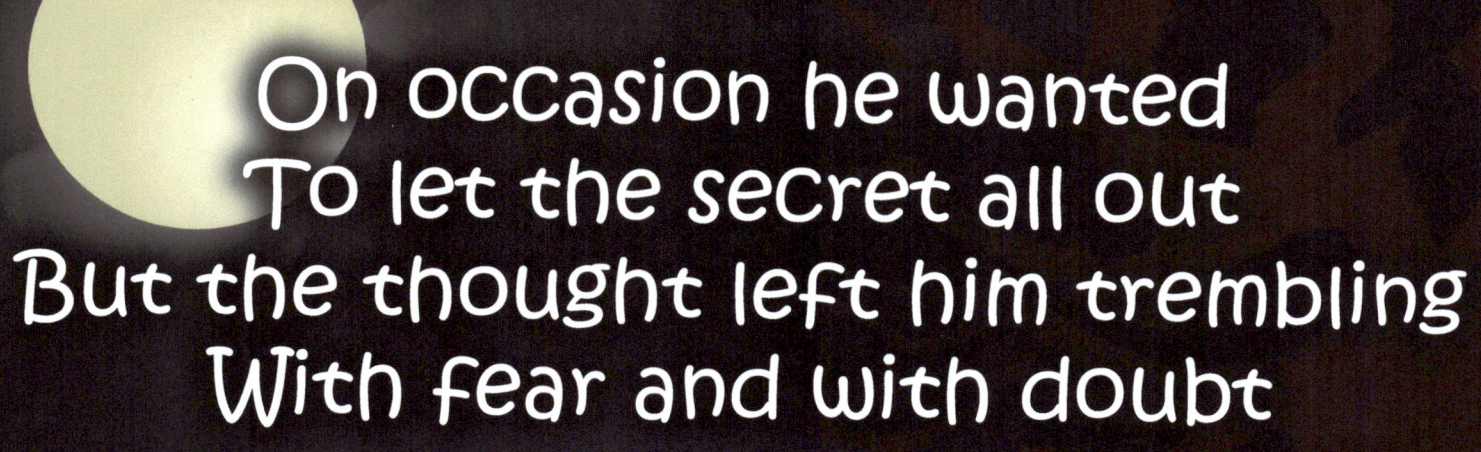

So to run from the fear
And to run from the shame
He buried the thought
To keep his good name

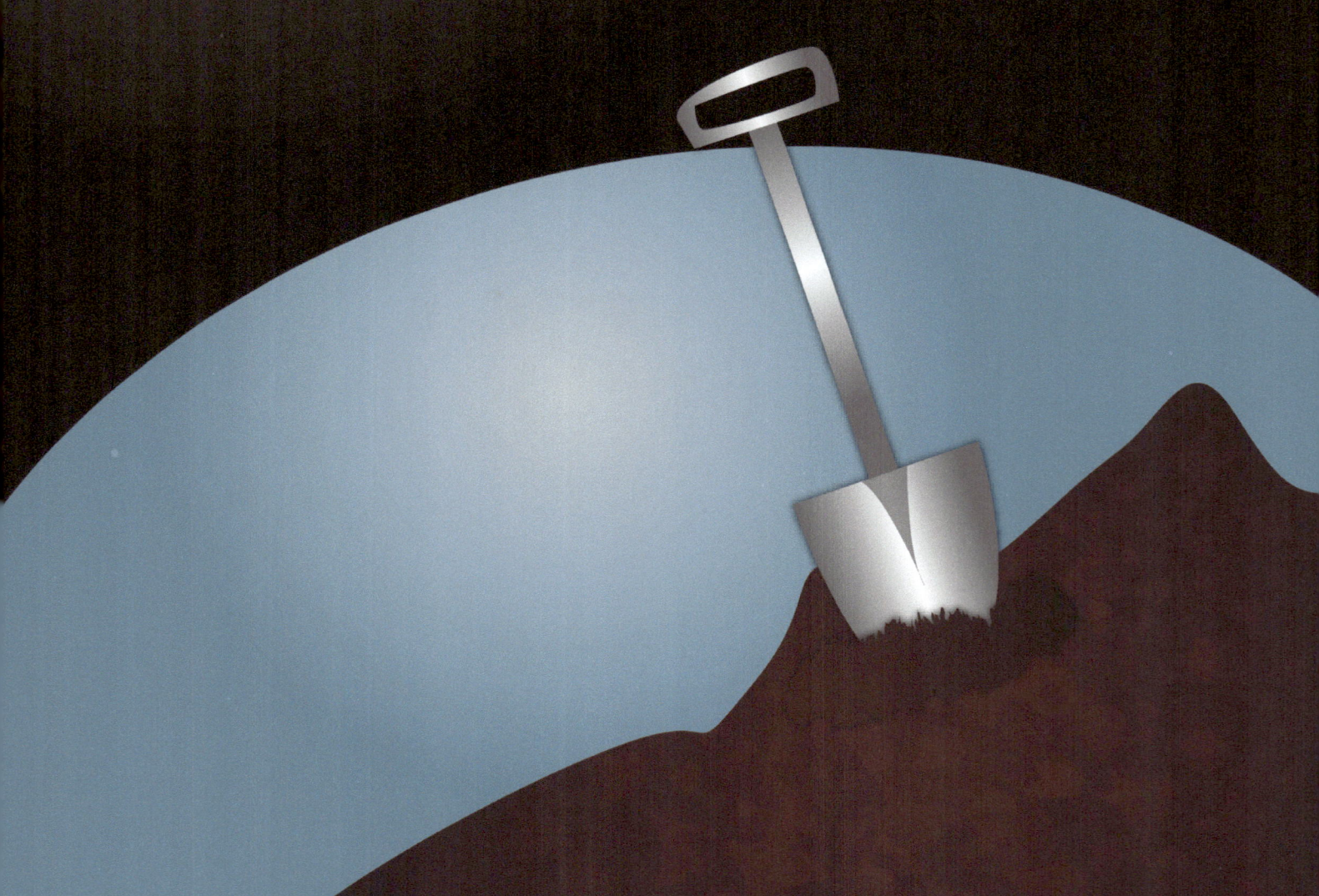

He disguised the hole's mouth
So it wouldn't look stranger
He neatly covered its path
And forgot of the danger

Every day that passed by
It got easier to dig
The hole was so deep now
So wide and so big

Still he played with his family
Each passing day
The blinders he wore
Seemed to make it ok

He laughed and he twirled
And he spun all around
Until one day his family
Was no where to be found

He had knocked them all down
Each one at a time
He wasn't aware
Of his shame or his crime

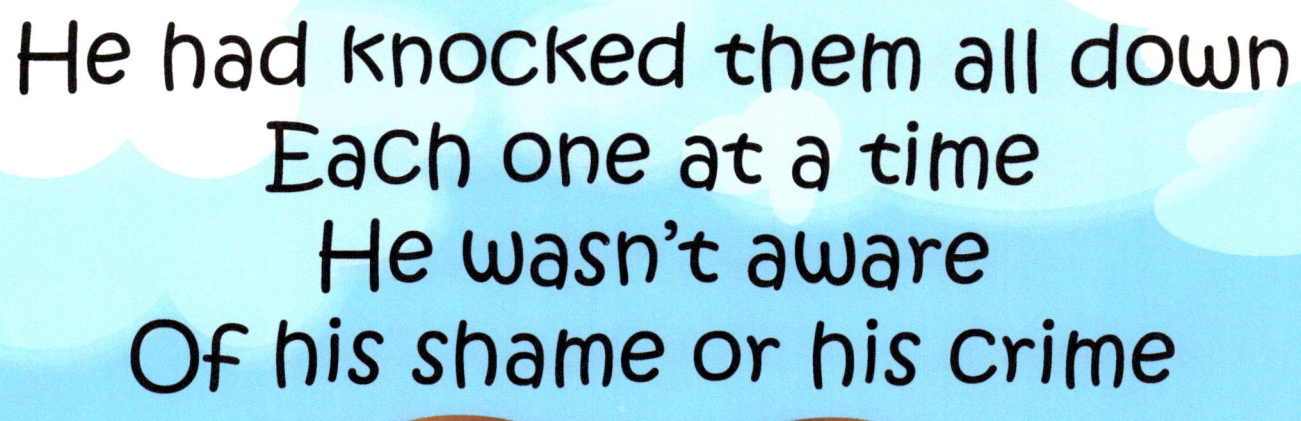

The family just sat in the hole
With the bugs and the snakes
They tried to be brave and just do
What it takes
So they begged and pleaded for him
To throw down a rope
They knew he could save them and
Give them some hope

Finally he threw down a rope
With much anger and spouting
"With one stipulation!" he kept
On shouting
They must do all that he wanted
And never again go away
He didn't understand
HE was the one
Who threw them away

They gladly most humbly
Agreed to the terms
The rope was thrown down
To the pit with the worms
Finally hope was soon in sight
...Then all of a sudden
  they were given a fright

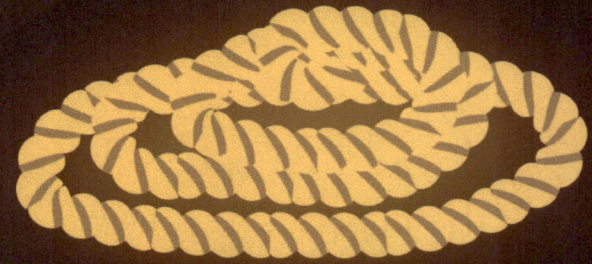

Not one end but two, came down
The deep well
He walked away proudly with
Nothing to tell
He walked away surely knowing
He had done all his part...
And nothing would change
His mind or his heart

Can you see that this boy
Doesn't think right at all?
He doesn't hear any warning
He doesn't heed any call

This is what happens
When you get addicted to things
It changes your mood
And how your mind thinks

Parent Guide

These are suggestions as you read this book.
It is up to you as the care giver to determine
What is right for your family.

This book is intended to be read with your child.
It is a tool to help you discuss the topic of addiction.
Consider the age of the child and consider whether
Or not the child is ready for the subject.

Use the scriptures provided here to talk about
God's good plan for our lives and what
Happens when we go astray.

Watch for cues from your child to determine
Readiness. Give them time to talk and ask
Questions as you read.

Educating your child on specific
addiction Issues early is better
than damage control later.

Scriptures

Matthew 6:22-23 New International Version (NIV)
22 "The eye is the lamp of the body. If your eyes are healthy,[a] your whole body will be full of light. 23 But if your eyes are unhealthy,[b] your whole body will be full of darkness. If then the light within you is darkness, how great is that darkness!

1st John 2:16
16 For everything in the world—the lust of the flesh, the lust of the eyes, and the pride of life—comes not from the Father but from the world.

Luke 8:17
For there is nothing hidden that will not be disclosed, and nothing concealed that will not be known or brought out into the open.

Ephesians 5:18
Don't be drunk with wine, because that will ruin your life. Instead, be filled with the Holy Spirit,

Proverbs 7:22
All at once he followed her
   like an ox going to the slaughter,
like a deer[a] stepping into a noose[b]
23
   till an arrow pierces his liver,
like a bird darting into a snare,
   little knowing it will cost him his life.

Written by Amy Norris
Illustrated by
Alexis Olguin & Amy Norris
© 2017 Reservation of Rights
ISBN-13: 978-0692939390
ISBN-10: 0692939393
TBT Ministries Inc. NPO
www.trainupachildministries.com